SNATCHES

Alec Cairncross

SNATCHES

COLIN SMYTHE
1980

First published in 1980 *by*
COLIN SMYTHE LTD.
PO Box 6, Gerrards Cross,
Buckinghamshire SL9 7AE

British Library Cataloguing in Publication Data
Cairncross, *Sir* Alec
Snatches.
I. Title
821'.9'14   PR6053.A36/

ISBN 0-86140-051-8

Printed in England by
Skelton's Press Ltd, Wellingborough, Northamptonshire.

Contents

The fragments of verse included here were written many years ago (none later than 1946). They are for the most part jottings, often incomplete, to recall a theme or a mood _ momentary diversions from a life absorbed in other things, combustible material snatched from the fire.

I THE PHONEY PEACE

Lines in a photograph album after a motor tour of the USA

Two armoured knights in an ironic age
Kill time in camera on a distant stage.
Here memory springs rich-flowering from the slain
And time annihilated lives again.

1936

Covenanting Country

In this wide moorland fringed with dirty haze
Voices fall quivering on the windless air;
The lazy seagulls trace a circling maze,
And pompous crows glean what the reapers spare.
Here the hot sky is empty of all rancour;
The quiet rivers wash away pretence.
Is this deep-rooted land a natural anchor
To peaceful living and secure good sense?
This is the home of ancient persecution,
Ungovernable wills, the spirit of denial,
Fanaticism. Men went to execution
'As to a marriage', mocking at their trial.
And we, who purpose with a calmer mind –
Can we be as implacable, less blind?

1937

Nutberry Hill

How long shall I hear larks in an empty sky
Or walk familiar hills against the sun?
When shall I ever again be able to lie
Outstretched by the headwaters where they run
Down everlastingly towards the sea?
The warm uncounted moments idly hum
Into the past: the satisfied mind spins free
With the sense of achievement: slow sounds come
Lazily over the valley, mingling with the scent
Of heather and the soft, black peat below.
Yet soon through this wide-arching firmament
Will come the laden messengers of death
Spewing from crowded skies a fouler breath
Than old, unskilled Vesuvius long ago.

1938

To G. C. Maclaurin
Killed at Madrid, Christmas 1936

You that have died courageous to the last
Who for a little while were raised from dust
To fight and vanish; you, whose forms were cast
In the same mould as ours, felt the same lust
For life, resolved great things as we do, dreamed,
Yourselves creatures of dreams: you chose the strife –
The merciless killing of adversaries seemed
Your duty. Scorning to jingle the loose coin of life
In Fascist pockets, you quickly paid the debt
In which we all are cradled. When you went,
Pregnant of victory to a dull death, you set
A living message on Death's instrument:
Freedom is fed upon the lives of men
Who, having freedom, yield it up again.

1938

Munich

A wilful, credulous, obstinate, old man
Decked in the honour of dishonoured friends
Parades betrayal as a novel plan
For everlasting peace, and makes amends
For Britain's misdeeds with Bohemian land:
Venting atonement on disarmed allies,
And finding justice, by some sleight of hand,
In yielding to injustice. Men of lies
Have had their way. Henceforward we are bound
As junior partners on the side of error.
We must watch helpless from unhallowed ground
Who might have won delivery from the Terror.
Uncrucified, you bring us others' sorrow
And shame that former Gods were wont to borrow!

1938

II THE PHONEY WAR AND AFTER

Whom then are we to salute, being about to die?
Are we too proud to name the masters that we serve?
Or is there no-one to lead us, none to sustain and inspirit
But these old men with their hard vision, harder self-esteem?

January 1940

The lights that shine in London town
Are not the lights of yester year:
Gay carnations in the sky
To tell us what and where to buy;
Highways bordered red and brown
Thrusting outwards like a spear
Patchworks of unshuttered light
Hung in rows throughout the night.

February 1940

Gold is gone out of the sky
And fled to the tiny stars;
Along deserted waterways
Brightness flickers and chars.

Tree skeletons raise bony hands
In avenues of belted white:
Leafless, unstirred, implacable,
Drained of colour, full of light.

March 1940

The lustre has gone from the evening sky
And all the marrow is out of my bones
And it's Oh for a month of leisure to lie
On a far hillside that nobody owns.

May 1940

The endless wheel of days goes round;
The air is heavy, the rain will come.
Our kindred are gone underground
And all the singing birds are dumb.

August 1940

The trees will soon be bare and drab
The air is sweet with the scent of death
Ah! Shield us! Shield us from the stab
Of memory quickened by autumn's breath.

October 1941

Luftwaffe

The things that prowl beneath the stars
Are beautiful behind their bars,
Stifling malignity acquired
From puppyish frisks we once admired.

November 1941

Moscow

Blow, winter wind, with keener gust:
Whistle and bite, blow your fill!
Blow our doubts to their distrust
Freeze them till their marrows rust,
Shatter and scourge, cleanse and kill.

Blow by day and blow by night
Rage and roar, whistle and bite.

December 1941

Again the haze of summer with the trees
Still bare along the twigs; pasture upturned
Through all the Eastern plain, fallow and drab,
Or bursting into green; the throbbing sky
Bearing its silver freight on reins of white.
Six winters past, six springs and still far underground
Life pushes upwards through the waterless earth.

Spring 1945

III THE MINISTRY OF AIRCRAFT PRODUCTION

Pale for a season, red for a day;
Nose to the grindstone, whiff of May;
Big decisions in little places,
And little decisions in finicky phrases;
Last year's minutes with this year's buds;
Youthful impatience with eminent duds;
Music-hall nightmares on telephone wires,
And truce-making talks because nobody fires.

Smith Square

There was a whispered scent of roses
Before the ice had broken and fled;
Crimson and cream in silken posies
Through the corridor ovens where bureaucrats tread.

And blackbirds sang in the frozen square
A Te Deum from gibbet boughs
By the roofless church that Wren built there
For Churchill's queen and Churchill's spouse.

Children of calamity
Called upon to plan
In what fearful amity
Bottlenecks we scan.

Our days are noon and midnight: without dawn
To lay cold hands upon the meadow grass
And beat back darkness till the world's astir;
Or dusk to soften sound and trim the sky
With crimson.

Our days are noon and midnight: but not now
A spreading noonday full of lazy sound;
Or candled midnight in a quiet room,
Mozart to lull the ear, and for the eye,
Mahogany and shadow.

Our days are noon and midnight: a perpetual noon
Of heat and clamour in a scentless summer;
While private meditations stand unwalled
And violate to the dust of business rubble,
Dingy in sun.

Our days are noon and midnight: with no rest
In darkness that revolves with freighted scoops
Of frivolous nightmares from the day before;
Crouching and waiting, waiting till the sky
Dawns without blood.

We are the prisoners, we are the judges,
Sentenced before we were called to the bar:
Summoned to penance for ancient grudges,
Night and day with the powers of a czar.

For us the banquets, for us the skilly,
The windowless club and the windowed gaol:
The exultation; the vain, the chilly
Grasp on the irremoveable rail.

We are the mothers when earth is pastureless
Forced to give suck to offspring unseen:
We are the men who wander masterless
Through desert dominions where none has been.

We must be deaf and blind and mute,
Hear as we falter the distant weeping,
See later slaughter and not refute
For all our jests, the voice unsleeping.

Windabout and windabout
Some go in and some come out.

They put four walls around me
To shut me from the sun
Between deep files they ground me
Until my work was done.

All day the bells kept ringing
Cries of imprisoned djinn
That on release sent winging
Tales deadlier than the din.

From cell to cell fermenting,
Hint, rumour and surmise,
Fed on misrepresenting
Half-understood replies,

Swelled with the iridescence
Of plausible – absurd
Until the bubbling nonsense
Exploded at a word.

IV   BERLIN, 1945-46

Between the walls of rubble everywhere
The timber drones propel their creaking loads,
Cold, tired and thin.
Leaves lie thick on the ground
Soon the frosts will begin.
City of desolation and despair.

City of endless music and ringing bells,
Funerals and farewells:
Terminus and transit mess
Babylon in modern dress.

Potsdam[1]

If four should join to frame a plan
For taking all the loot they can
While leaving to a fifth enough
Of all the necessary stuff
To just maintain but not exceed
The average of Europe's need:
Always omitting from the sum
(What may appear a trifle rum)
The bear and lion as extremes
Beyond the reach of Europe's dreams . . . .

★

Then take your glass and raise it high
To Luba and the reason why
We all assemble every day
To while the idle hours away
As we absorb the rule of Four
And think of 1984.

[1]Original given in Berlin to Luba Model in 1946 and now lost.

V LIFE AND DEATH

Merry-go-round

Make way! Make way! On the wheel that turns,
The wheel that turns and is always still.
Pass on! On to the fire that burns
With flames perpetually chill.

The dead that live within our soul
Shall live again when we are gone;
And they and we re-write the scroll
In characters that fate hands on.

When I was young, you were my fathers;
When I am old, you'll be my sons.
The fullnesses a lifetime gathers
Exceed the span a lifetime runs.

Make way! Make way! On the wheel that turns,
The wheel that turns and is always still.
Pass on! On to the fire that burns
With flames perpetually chill.

1937

Flux

The living are the fragments of the dead
In Time's kaleidoscope for ever shaken;
Children of chaos unto order wed,
By law created and by law forsaken.

The woods take colour from the year's decay
And beauty hangs upon the dying leaves,
Dancing in tremulous bravery to display
The immortal vigour that Time's sickle cleaves.

In the slow fire of living we are doomed,
Even as the earth must perish of its heat:
But as earth's fires in spring are many-wombed,
So we, in love, accomplish Time's defeat.

Come then, my love, and let us be
At one with Time, which is our enemy.

1938

Incendiaries

Within the within we acknowledge
Shadows only; symbols abide and rhythms
And harmonies unanswerable to knowledge.

Substantial things command no present homage
Till out of dreams and remembrance, threads of mortality,
We fashion awareness to screen and exalt.

Rainbow and blossom possess and elude us:
We clutch at thin veils in the sky, the gay colours vanish;
Pluck the delicate flower, it withers away.

Shadows have names but named they cease to be shadows.
If we would call, it must be soft from afar;
The whisper carries, the shouting falters and dies.

We wrap the present in words, mastering it,
Letting it fizzle over the sands of articulation.
But grief and love and terror still blaze through
To the primitive quick where language has no station.

1942

The Power and the Glory

I

We do not bow to wood and stone
Nor anything we do not own;
Our hopes of joy do not extend
To anything we cannot spend.
Yet idols compass us about:
Look in the glass and one looks out,
Gibbering assurances of grace
From anxious eyes and suppliant face.
Or hearken to the Voice of God
Measuring out our days in quod
From every mantelpiece and steeple
Preaching obedience to the people.
Or watch the drum's domestication
In drawing-room perambulation –
Tribute to deities unseen
Behind the radio's fretted screen.

II

We need no priests to chide our sins
With lofty words and private grins
Nor theologians to expound
Why God requires us underground.
Yet still we offer up our prayers
In shrill returns of our affairs,
Accepting benison from hands
Stronger than Providence commands.
And heretics are soundly whipped
For certainties too firmly gripped
Of quick or ultimate salvation
Outwith the rulers of the nation.
For in a people born in doubt
Original sin, if not cast out
With all the violence of fear,
Must leave no rulers to revere.

III

Therefore rejoice that we agree
On our dissimilarity,
And rally to destroy the knaves
Worshipped abroad by fellow-slaves.

VI LOVE

Love is not blind but dumb;
We speak and no words come
Till echo answers back.
Another voice supplies
Songs that we recognise
In harmonies we lack.

I am content that you should go from me:
That those sad eyes which shyly stared at mine
Should stare no more: your importunity
Of breasts cease heaving at my touch: your line
Of scarlet lips beseech in vain: your heart
Pound daily its regrets. You cannot sway
My pity to your service now by art,
Nor strike in my eyes what your own convey.
How can I pity knowing that I take
From your swift-dwindling storehouse what might bind
With ties that time's unwindings would not break
A truer lover and a nobler mind.
Believe me dead: my bitter ashes burned,
Seek love again and find your love returned.

If life is short, why do you shorten it
With triflings that you know are counterfeit?
You preach to make me more importunate
And force me cringe in love to your conceit.
If I could love and cease to love at will
I would not give myself to your disdain
Nor idly chafe until I had my fill
Of casual kisses and ecstatic pain.
How can I leave you for an empty world
In which no passion stirs to quicken mine?
Must all desire perpetually be furled
And day give way to day without design?
Take what you will of me: I cannot live
Till you, my master, cherish what I give.

I dreamt that you were silver;
I dreamt that you were gold;
I dreamt that you were cloud and sky
Over mountains five miles high
And never would grow old.

I dreamt that you were summer;
I dreamt that you were spring;
The water-meadows in a swoon,
Larks singing in the afternoon,
And every perfect thing.

But ah! my dreams were cruel,
And oh! my dreams were true:
For we may love but cannot please
Things of beauty such as these
Impervious to our view.

Others have sung your beauty: why should I
Hackney your praises
While our successive laureates multiply
With choicer phrases,
Recording without air of prophecy
What now amazes?

You were the first of women in whose hair
The serpent coiled;
By foreign shores you met Ulysses' stare
While home he toiled;
Sheba and Naufretête you were there
In times unspoiled.

Earth touches us with questions we can claim
No answer to;
Moved we invent and struggle for a name
That will subdue.
O, lovely one, in you reside the same
Riddle and clue.

There have been times when memory's flimsy net
Could take no fleeting mermaid catch of you;
While dark in sunken caves beneath the blue
Insistency of things, closed to the fret
Of recollection you lay hid entombed,
Until for sesame I called some day
We shared, reviving your enchantment's sway,
In talk and jest and journeyings resumed,
To raise your bright-eyed shadow from the gloom.
Then some vestigial thing within the soul,
Unanswerable to memory's control,
Stirred, and Aphrodite rose, outlined
In beauty, flooding gold across the mind
Like sunshine filling a high-windowed room.

I cannot look on beauty but I find
Instant remembrancers: each form, each face
Contents and troubles so it brings to mind
Some trick of carriage or some show of grace
That I have seen in you. My fancy takes
Earth's rind for palette, for your canvas, sky
Sun-daubed and full of freshness. No scene breaks
Virgin on my enjoyment through an eye
Sophisticate and fecund; but comes stamped
With your insignia from empty dawn
And the gold warp of noon until dusk lamped
With silver and a hundred eyes. Beauty must fawn
When greater beauty queens it in our heart
Corrupting peace, once beauty's counterpart.

How shall we say what our hearts are singing
When words are snakes that twist in our hands?
How enchant them to living trophies
That dance fulfilment of our commands?

We fly too fast to hit our passion:
Though we draw on the inner core of things,
Words resist, and the curves they fashion
Veer away from our displaced wings.

How shall we love without deceiving
When what is told is a thing that is not;
And the thing that is is past conceiving
In words hot-forged but no longer hot.

O wind that sets the cornfields singing
And somersaults the laden bee
Mix with carillons you're bringing
From apple-bells in fullness ringing
A message to my love from me.

Blown is the wild rose, blown the thorn;
Dog-hips fatten in glossy red;
Bramble and briony adorn
Hedges that enclose the corn
Within its golden bed.

Say as you shake the blossom down,
Laburnum, lavender and rose:
Say that beauty is a crown
Long outlasting any gown
Fashioned for a queenly pose.

Tell her, wind that lives in her hair
Rainbowed as it leaves her shoulders
Beauty is not half so fair
Lacking promise of an heir
And returns when blossom moulders.

I am too proud, lascivious and weak
For you to love me: too irresolute
And fearful of inconstancy to speak
The moment's passion, or in long pursuit
Take issue with my doubts. In you there sits
Serenity of purpose and desire
Clad in the complete beauty that befits
The union of simplicity and fire.
You should be matched with equal strength and calm
Not with a tame and shallow hesitance.
Yet though you cannot love me as I am,
Touch me with hope of quick deliverance
And I shall catch your pattern of delight
As flowers win colour from returning light.

There is a shape and colour that the mind
Gives to the past; each act is overlaid
By memory's brush and fitted undesigned
Into a frame wherein we see displayed
A retrospective glory. We transmute
Ancient discomfort to a present joy
Compass our years in little and commute
Profounder sorrows and delights that cloy.
In the unfolding of this new-born past
No cataract ever shall obscure my sight
Of distant Appletrewick when with hair
Down-dropped, bare shoulders gleaming white,
You waited by the Wharfe and waiting cast
Eternal magic on the autumn air.

Shimmering the moments when we are moved to yield
To unknown promptings and we strain to hear
What stirs in us, what oracle concealed
And dungeoned like the springs that disappear
In Pyrenean limestone far from view.
Through depths reverberating with the twang
Of lacerations without form or clue
Issues the muffled rhythm creation sang.
Whence come these moments? What has power to raise
The sleeping singer from her inner couch
And touch eternal things with wonder? Is it not
Some special beauty that demands our praise,
Nostalgia that opens memory's pouch
And half-awareness of a former lot?

All beautiful things, all I have loved, are no more than an echo
That sounds and re-echoes, my love, in longing for you:
The soft rain redolent of English earth
And rhododendrons plumed with Christmas snow;
The distant star alight at evening's birth;
Cold windless meadows white with morning dew;
Sleek pomp of stallions and proud necks of swans;
Tough stems of heather; and raw morning winds
Trailing mists from the streets; mountain dawns;
Rowan trees set in high gullies with their crop
Of crimson . . .

Decalogue over Two

Do not look across the sea
Until your sails are spread;
Board no ship by bay or quay
That does not wait your tread.

Pluck no roses in the dark
You will not see by day;
Perfume leaves a deadlier mark
When nothing shows but gray.

Never come again by paths
That bloom and once were bare;
Feet that chill in dewey baths
Must walk with tiptoe care.

Do not heap upon the fire
More than flame will catch;
Emptying scuttles to acquire
Haste without despatch.

If it be not yea or nay
Ask yet ten times more.
Seek to enter by a way
That none has tried before.

VII OLD AGE

Salutation to Grandpa Cairncross on his eightieth birthday

Hail! Chieftain of the Cairncross Clan,
The Grandpapa of Frances Anne!
Upon whose patriarchal face
Whiskers and goatee beard embrace.
This very day you have completed
Full fourscore years and, undefeated,
Enter on yet another score
As energetic as before.
What if you have acquired of late
No inconsiderable weight?
– Age pays a dividend in girth
As trees add rings each year from birth.
The hair that decorates your pow
May be more sparse and whiter now;
And grandparental eyes may need
The aid of spectacles to read.
Yet still they shine in evidence
Of firm good nature and good sense.
Your virtues I need no prolong
– In us less gloriously they throng,
And why enumerate the merits
Posterity in part inherits?
Enough that locally you may go
For uncrowned King of Lesmahagow,
And that you have a growing brood
Throughout the country. To conclude,
I send you our congratulations
And warm regards and salutations.
May you continue still to thrive
When past the age of ninety-five!

12.2.45